FOUR DOWNS TO A PRO FOOTBALL TRIVIA CHAMPION

BY CHRIS 51

For my brother,
And the sport that has bonded
us since our early childhood.

PREFACE

Unlike any football trivia book you have encountered before, these pages do not just revolve around multi-million dollar superstar quarterbacks. They span the whole field of players. Lifetime back-ups, one year wonders, #1 busts...they are all in here!

Every question enclosed is only about the players; the guys who make the team, not the teams themselves. The men putting themselves on the chalk line to entertain us every Sunday deserve their own book, and now they have this tribute.

Like the pros themselves, this book is not for the wimpy, it's tough, it will put up a fight, and it will take all of your mental strength to beat it. But, like the game itself, that's what makes it great!

ROSTER

INTRODUCTION

I am so tired of endlessly searching for a good football trivia book. The only books that I can ever score either encompass all sport genres, or are so easy that I finish them in one bathroom session!

I don't need anymore novels brimmed with questions on only superstar QB's that are a paragraph long and read like the old middle school math riddles; if train A leaves the station with two cars and train B, blah, blah, blah!

I am also bored with old-timers writing trivia books on only the good ole' players from their generation who would probably throw in their leather helmets if they ever got hit by the likes of a Lawrence Taylor or Reggie White.

Yes I am being absolutely cynical and even downright downtrodden, but I have earned my bad attitude over the years by spending my allowance money on boring and useless trivia rags.

In this book I ran a different route. After memorizing the backs of my Topps football cards for decades, I decided to put them to use. I started out by covering up players names with my thumb and guessing who they were just from teams, stats, or uniform numbers. Yes it

1

was completely nerdy, drove my wife insane, and was a total waste of time, but that's what made it so much fun.

I have taken it a yard further in this book by making the short questions into a game. Play alone and beat the best, or play it with a friend and humiliate them with your football genius. You can each take a separate page at a time and add your scores as you go, or just whip em' for the sport of it.

You have to know your players for this book. There are no team questions. There are no questions about franchise records, coaches, or Superbowls. These pages are dedicated to the players and the players only. Not just the superstars and Hall of Famers' either. We will get down and dirty diving into an array of athletes. We will rediscover forgotten heroes, one-year wonders, lifetime backups, and everyone else in between the hashes.

There will be no questions about the old-timers. We all respect them and we all appreciate the path that they paved to make the game become what it is today. But, we all also know everything they have done and achieved, and we have all heard it hundreds of times in

hundreds of formats. The trivia on the following pages is from 1970 to today. When the AFL-NFL merger transpired, it united the players and cemented their accomplishments. Competition was at its highest, and a new wave of records began to unfold.

All of the information and facts that I acquired for this endeavor was taken from my own personal Topps football card collection. After hundreds of grueling hours of training that would make even Jerry Rice seem lazy, I have compiled a collection of trivia that I hope will make the Topps card company proud, and repay them for the years of fun that I have had collecting their cards.

No Google or interwebbing was used in the making of this book. It is 100% old-school smash mouth writing and hard-earned knowledge.

I hope you enjoy reading or playing it as much as I did making it.

Go pro or go home!

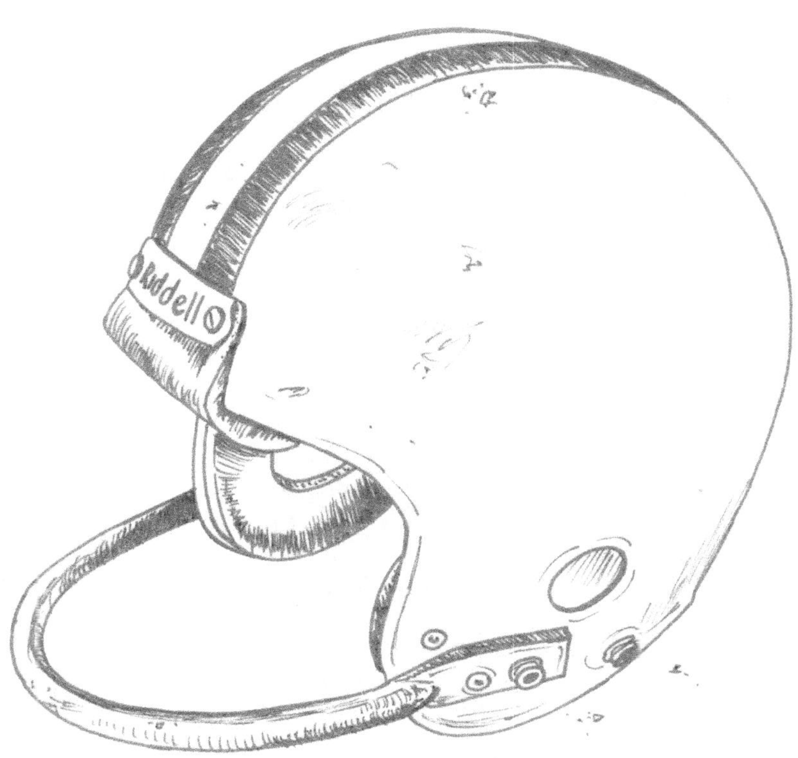

PLAYBOOK

(Instructions)

The rules are simple. The quicker you answer the question, the more points you get.

• Take a bookmark, piece of paper, or even your thumb, and cover all of the lines so that only one clue is exposed at a time. If you can't score on the first clue, move your blocker down slightly to expose the second clue, then the third, and so on.

• Write down your guess of the player in the space provided, then circle the clue number where you guessed it.

• When you finish a page or a chapter you can refer to the back of the book for the answers. If you answered correctly, write the point total next to your player in the space provided. The top of each new chapter page has a scorecard to help you.

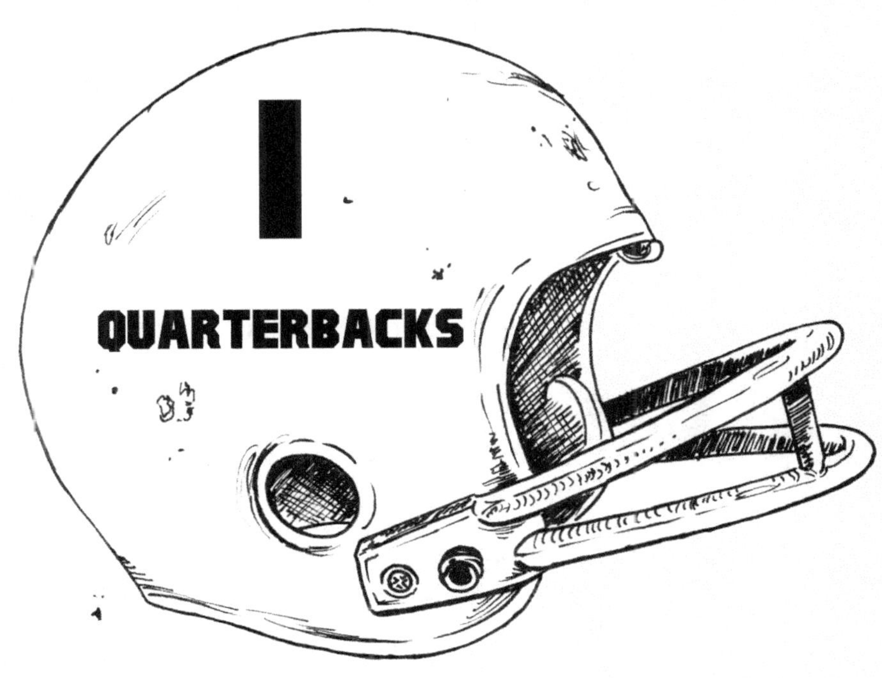

The most glamerous position in any sport is the QB. It takes brains and braun, toughness and finess, courage and sacrifice.

Below you will find a wild roster of quarterback questions. Everyone from Hall of Famers, to gunslingers, #1 picks to total busts, and career backups to one-hit wonders.

Refer to the following point scale for all questions (except extra credit at chapter conclusion).

1st down...7 points
(Getting correct answer on first clue only)
2nd down...3 points
(Needing first two clues to get correct answer)
3rd down...2 points
(Needing first three clues to get correct anser)
4th down...1 point
(Needing all four clues to get correct answer)

1st...Defunct Milton (College)
2nd...Not drafted
3rd...#17
4th...Seahawks
Player:_______________________________Pts:_____

1st...Single-bar facemask
2nd...L.T. victim
3rd...Redskins
4th...ESPN
Player:_______________________________ Pts:_____

1st...USFL star
2nd...Curly-hair
3rd...1985 rookie
4th...Silent "H"
Player:_______________________________ Pts:_____

1st...Utah (University)
2nd...Heisman hopeful
3rd...#1 Pick
4th...49ers
Player:_______________________________ Pts:_____

1st...Buccaneers drafted
2nd...Superbowl
3rd...BYU scrambler
4th...#8
Player:_______________________________ Pts:_____

1st...#12
2nd..."Failure to Launch"
3rd...Blonde Bomber
4th...Fox Gameday
Player:_______________________________ Pts:_____

1st...#10 lefty
2nd...Redskin coach
3rd...Scrambler
4th...Inaugural Hawk
Player:_________________ Pts:_____

1st...Sunglasses
2nd...Attitude
3rd...Headband
4th...Bears
Player:_________________ Pts:_____

1st...Hurricanes
2nd...Cowboys
3rd...Dolphins
4th...Browns
Player:_________________ Pts:_____

1st...Oregon Duck
2nd...#12
3rd...#1 Pick
4th...Atlanta
Player:_________________ Pts:_____

1st...Grambling
2nd...African American
3rd...Superbowl MVP
4th...Buccaneers
Player:_________________ Pts:_____

1st...1983 UCLA
2nd...4000+ yards 1986
3rd...Raiders
4th...Redskins
Player:_________________ Pts:_____

13

1st…Alcorn State
2nd…"Air"
3rd…Ravens
4th…Oilers
Player:________________ Pts:_____

14

1st…Cowboys drafted 1977
2nd…Buccaneers
3rd…Chiefs
4th…49ers
Player:________________ Pts:_____

15

1st…"The King"
2nd…Michigan
3rd…6'5"
4th…49ers
Player:________________ Pts:_____

16

1st…Bearded
2nd…Oregon Duck
3rd…1973 rookie
4th…Lifetime Charger
Player:________________ Pts:_____

17

1st…Grocery store packer
2nd…Cut by Packers
3rd…Arena League
4th…Superbowl MVP
Player:________________ Pts:_____

18

1st…1986 Heisman
2nd…Brooklyn boy
3rd…Hurricanes
4th…Jets
Player:________________ Pts:_____

19
1st...#21
2nd...6-Time All Pro
3rd...1970
4th...San Diego
Player:_______________________ Pts:______

20
1st...Oilers drafted 1986
2nd...Purdue
3rd...Saints
4th...Rams
Player:_______________________ Pts:______

21
1st...Yankees organization
2nd...Colts drafted 1983
3rd...Stanford
4th...#7
Player:_______________________ Pts:______

22
1st...Albino Blonde
2nd...Autistic son
3rd...Jets
4th...Bengals
Player:_______________________ Pts:______

23
1st...2nd QB Pick 1992
2nd...Notre Dame golden boy
3rd...Big bust
4th...Seattle
Player:_______________________ Pts:______

24
1st...22nd Pick 2003
2nd...2004 knee Injury
3rd...2002 Gator
4th...Bears
Player:_______________________ Pts:______

25
1st…1998 Ducks
2nd…Common last name
3rd…#1 Pick
4th…Bengals bust
Player:_________________ Pts:_____

26
1st…Walter Andrew
2nd…3rd round 1986
3rd…#7
4th…Steelers
Player:_________________ Pts:_____

27
1st…1st to 4000 yards
2nd…Greatest Upset
3rd…"Broadway"
4th…#12
Player:_________________ Pts:_____

28
1st…Marino back-up
2nd…Team records
3rd…32 TD's 1995
4th…Lions
Player:_________________ Pts:_____

29
1st…Browns
2nd…Little League W.S. champ
3rd…1972 draft
4th…4000+ yards 1980
Player:_________________ Pts:_____

30
1st…1989 Heisman
2nd…Bust
3rd…14 NCAA records
4th…Lions
Player:_________________ Pts:_____

31
1st…"Magic Man"
2nd…10th Round 1987
3rd…NFL leader 1989
4th…Before Favre
Player:_________________ Pts:_____

32
1st…1987 National Champ
2nd…Hurricane
3rd…Cowboy
4th…Saint
Player:_________________ Pts:_____

33
1st…1983 Buccaneers
2nd…"Throwin' Samoan"
3rd…#1 Pick
4th…Bengals
Player:_________________ Pts:_____

34
1st…Soup mom
2nd…Syracuse
3rd…240 Lb. QB
4th…Eagles
Player:_________________ Pts:_____

35
1st…1961 rookie
2nd…Redskins drafted
3rd…5 TD game 1969
4th…Eagles records
Player:_________________ Pts:_____

36
1st…1988 Heisman runner-up
2nd…Oakland A's drafted (twice)
3rd…Trojan
4th…Lions
Player:_________________ Pts:_____

37

1st... 1984 rookie
2nd...7 year back-up
3rd...Raiders
4th...Relieved Simms
Player:________________ Pts:_____

38

1st...2004 Arena League R.O.Y.
2nd...Seminoles
3rd...African American
4th...Saints drafted
Player:________________ Pts:_____

39

1st...1970 Heisman
2nd...Stanford hero
3rd...Patriots #1 Pick
4th...Longtime Raider
Player:________________ Pts:_____

40

1st...Panthers #1
2nd...Saints
3rd...Giants
4th...Raiders
Player:________________ Pts:_____

41

1st...Rewrote Oilers records
2nd...#1 Pick 1971
3rd...Raiders
4th...#7
Player:________________ Pts:_____

42

1st...Ravens rookie
2nd...Cal 2002
3rd...6'-3", 234 Lbs.
4th...#8
Player:________________ Pts:_____

1st... 1984 rookie
2nd...7 year back-up
3rd...Raiders
4th...Relieved Simms
Player:_________________ Pts:_____

1st...2004 Arena League R.O.Y.
2nd...Seminoles
3rd...African American
4th...Saints drafted
Player:_________________ Pts:_____

1st...1970 Heisman
2nd...Stanford hero
3rd...Patriots #1 Pick
4th...Longtime Raider
Player:_________________ Pts:_____

1st...Panthers #1
2nd...Saints
3rd...Giants
4th...Raiders
Player:_________________ Pts:_____

1st...Rewrote Oilers records
2nd...#1 Pick 1971
3rd...Raiders
4th...#7
Player:_________________ Pts:_____

1st...Ravens rookie
2nd...Cal 2002
3rd...6'-3", 234 Lbs.
4th...#8
Player:_________________ Pts:_____

49

1st...11 year Ram
2nd...5 year Eagle
3rd..."Not singer Peter"
4th...Type of catholic
Player:_________________ Pts:_____

50

1st...18 year Cardinal
2nd...#17
3rd...1974-77 Pro-Bowler
4th...Retired a Redskin
Player:_________________ Pts:_____

51

1st...(In order) Jaguars
2nd...Bills
3rd...Buccs
4th...Redskins
Player:_________________ Pts:_____

52

1st...1995 Gator
2nd...1996 Bear
3rd...2002 Redskin
4th...2004 Bill
Player:_________________ Pts:_____

53

1st...#14
2nd...Two-bar black facemask
3rd...32,838 career yards
4th...16 year Bengal
Player:_________________ Pts:_____

54

1st...Mid-90's Bengal
2nd...Jets drafted
3rd...2 year Saint
4th...African American
Player:_________________ Pts:_____

55

1st...#1 Pick Bronco bust
2nd...5 year NFL absence
3rd...Arena League
4th...XFL
Player:_________________ Pts:_____

56

1st...11 year early Lion
2nd...21 rushing TD's
3rd...15 year career
4th..."Not Tom"
Player:_________________ Pts:_____

57

1st...Superbowl Charger
2nd...(3) 3000 yard years
3rd...Louisiana native
4th...Redskin risk
Player:_________________ Pts:_____

58

1st...1999 #1 Pick
2nd...UCLA hero
3rd...Chicago villain
4th...486 career yards
Player:_________________ Pts:_____

59

1st...14 year Dolphin
2nd...Retired a Brown
3rd...#10
4th...Career back-up
Player:_________________ Pts:_____

60

1st...Bearded #7
2nd...15 year vet
3rd...ESPN
4th..."Jaws"
Player:_________________ Pts:_____

1st...Ram before Warner
2nd...Redskins
3rd...Texans
4th...Ravens
Player:_________________ Pts:_____

1st...12 year Bill
2nd...#12
3rd...1973 rookie
4th...17 year mainstay
Player:_________________ Pts:_____

1st...Also a punter
2nd...#11
3rd...WFL Memphis
4th...Cowboy
Player:_________________ Pts:_____

1st...Mr. Oregon Duck
2nd...#3
3rd...3rd overall Pick
4th...Lions
Player:_________________ Pts:_____

1st...1993 San Diego 8th rounder
2nd...1997 Redskin rookie
3rd...2000 Ram
4th...2006 Chiefs Vet
Player:_________________ Pts:_____

1st...1974 N.Y.-Char WFL
2nd...1975 Chicago WFL
3rd...1976 Lions rookie
4th...1988 Browns back-up
Player:_________________ Pts:_____

67

1st...#1 Pick 1986
2nd...Lions longtime hopeful
3rd...Lions 23 game bust
4th...1990 Ram bench rider
Player:_________________ Pts:_____

68

1st...Bengal bust
2nd...1992 #1 Pick
3rd...U of Houston
4th...Retired a Raider
Player:_________________ Pts:_____

69

1st...1991 Hurricane
2nd...1992 Buccaneer
3rd...1995 Colt
4th...1996 Dolphin
Player:_________________ Pts:_____

70

1st...Bears 1981 starter
2nd...8 year Raider
3rd...USC
4th...African American QB
Player:_________________ Pts:_____

71

1st...Broncos #7
2nd...Pre-Elway
3rd...Cowboys #1 Pick
4th...18 year vet
Player:_________________ Pts:_____

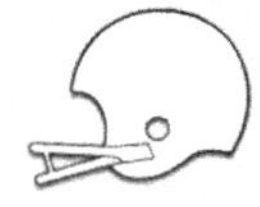 **EXTRA CREDIT** 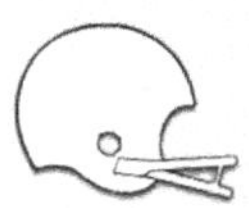

Extra Credit Questions are more challenging, therefore worth more points. Most of these players were in the league for only a short time, were low draftees, career back-ups, or just ranked in the unknown. But, they were all still pros. These are the answers that will make you a trivia pro.

Refer to the following point scale for all questions.
1st down...7 points
(Getting correct answer on first clue only)
2nd down...3 points
(Needing first two clues to get correct answer)
3rd down...2 points
(Needing first three clues to get correct anser)
4th down...1 point
(Needing all four clues to get correct answer)

72
1st...1994 Arizona St. starter
2nd...1995 Bears 7th RD Pick
3rd...1996-97 Colts part-timer
4th...1998 Bengals back-up
Player:_________________ Pts:_____

73
1st...Leinhart's college back-up
2nd...Brady's back-up
3rd...USC pitcher
4th..."Not a Sand..."
Player:_________________ Pts:_____

74
1st...6'-8"
2nd...San Diego State
3rd...#1 bust
4th...Mark's brother
Player:_________________ Pts:_____

75
1st…Before Favre
2nd…Duke
3rd…1989 rookie
4th…Packers
Player:________________ Pts:_____

76
1st…Marino back-up
2nd…Virginia
3rd…1993 Patriot
4th…PAT holder
Player:________________ Pts:_____

77
1st…1989 Seminole
2nd…Uses middle name too
3rd…#10
4th…Bears
Player:________________ Pts:_____

78
1st…Texas Tech star
2nd…Uses middle name too
3rd…1989 2nd Round pick
4th…1990 Chargers
Player:________________ Pts:_____

79
1st…11 Year C.F.L starter
2nd…1974 rookie
3rd…Jacksonville State
4th…1985 Rams
Player:________________ Pts:_____

80
1st…1979 draftee
2nd…"Not a pickle"
3rd…Vikings
4th…1983 starter
Player:________________ Pts:_____

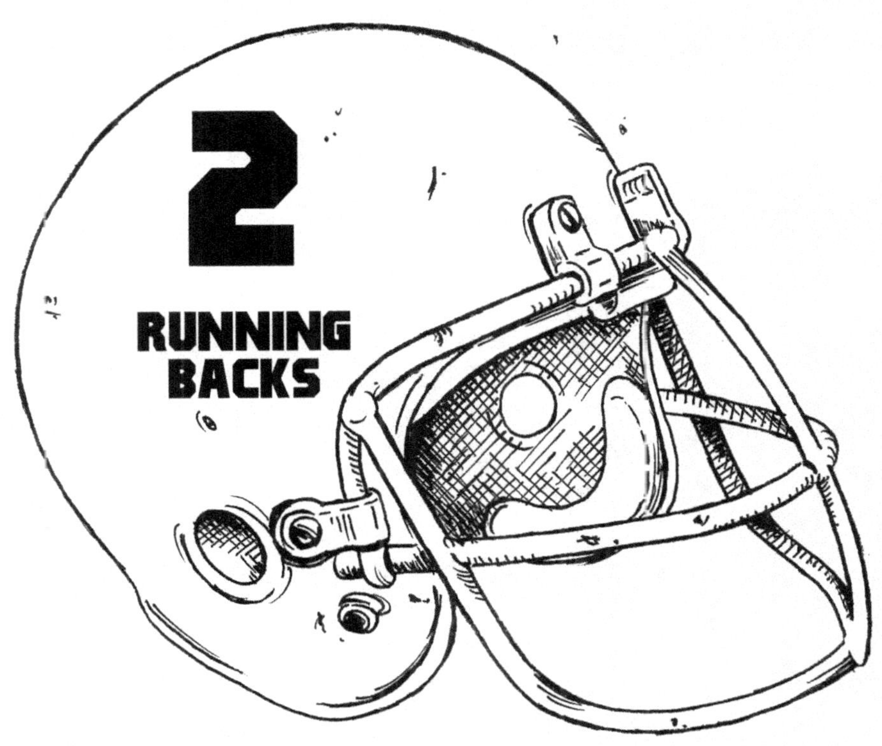

2
RUNNING BACKS

The most violent position in football is the running back. Taking bone-crushing hits every time you touch the ball is just another day at the office.

Below you will find a bruising roster of running back-questions. Everyone from Hall of Famers to one game wonders, 1000 yard rushers to career blockers, top draftees to total busts.

Refer to the following point scale for all questions (except extra credit at chapter conclusion).

1st down...7 points
(Getting correct answer on first clue only)
2nd down...3 points
(Needing first two clues to get correct answer)
3rd down...2 points
(Needing first three clues to get correct anser)
4th down...1 point
(Needing all four clues to get correct answer)

1st...2411 yards 1985
2nd...USFL
3rd...Bulldogs
4th...Dallas
Player:___________________ Pts:_____

1st..."Truck"
2nd...1000 tandem
3rd...#1 Pick 1984
4th...Browns
Player:___________________ Pts:_____

1st...Chargers drafted 1983
2nd...Texas A&M
3rd...Eagles
4th...Steelers
Player:___________________ Pts:_____

1st...1000 yard rookie 1989
2nd...Alabama
3rd...#26
 4th...Broncos
Player:___________________ Pts:_____

1st...Falcons
2nd...1979 rookie
3rd...4-Time 1000 yarder
4th...Auburn alumni
Player:___________________ Pts:_____

1st...Tampa Bay USFL
2nd...Jerry-curl
3rd...#1 Pick 1983
4th...San Diego
Player:___________________ Pts:_____

1st...3000+ yard Gator
2nd...1998 Draft
3rd...Tattoos
4th...Jaguars
Player:_________________ Pts:_____

1st...1980 Bruin
2nd...Led NFL in 1982
3rd...1983 Pro Bowler
4th...Jets
Player:_________________ Pts:_____

1st..."Little Train"
2nd...5'-6"
3rd...1000 yard receiver
4th...San Diego
Player:_________________ Pts:_____

1st...1986 AP Rookie of Year
2nd...Sandwich
3rd...Washington State
4th...New Orleans
Player:_________________ Pts:_____

1st...Rangers minor leagues
2nd...Ditka pick
3rd...Marijuana
4th...Dolphins
Player:_________________ Pts:_____

1st...#1 Pick 1988
2nd...253 Lb. fullback
3rd..."Ironhead"
4th...Saints
Player:_________________ Pts:_____

1st…A clear liquid
2nd…Notre Dame
3rd…#32
4th…Seahawk
Player:_____________________ Pts:_____

1st…1600+ yard rookie
2nd…"Mister"
3rd…#1 Pick 1981
4th…Redskins
Player:_____________________ Pts:_____

1st…"Dirty Bird"
2nd…1800+ yards 1998
3rd…Injuries
4th…Falcons
Player:_____________________ Pts:_____

1st…1000 yard RB & WR
2nd…1988 MVP
3rd…"Catfish"
4th…49ers
Player:_____________________ Pts:_____

1st…1992-95 1000 yarder
2nd…#42
3rd…Cowboys
4th…Seahawks records
Player:_____________________ Pts:_____

1st…Corn
2nd…1992 1000 yarder
3rd…Packers, Jets, Jags
4th…Buccaneers
Player:_____________________ Pts:_____

1st...#20
2nd...NFC R.O.Y.
3rd...1978 Heisman
4th...Injury killed career
Player:_________________ Pts:_____

1st...5'-7" Giant
2nd...Also kick-returner
3rd...Rookie Pro-Bowler
4th...Townson State
Player:_________________ Pts:_____

1st...2004 Pro-Bowl blocker
2nd...North Carolina
3rd...#33
4th...10+ year Packer
Player:_________________ Pts:_____

1st...NFL Leader 1970
2nd...#43
3rd...1st 1000 yarder of team
4th...Redskins
Player:_________________ Pts:_____

1st...1986-90 LSU
2nd...#1 Pick 1991
3rd...Chiefs
4th...Common last name
Player:_________________ Pts:_____

1st...3-Time Nebraska 1000 yarder
2nd...1981 Draft
3rd...Benjamin...
4th...Dolphins
Player:_________________ Pts:_____

1st...1400+ yards 1974
2nd...#1 Pick 1973
3rd...Purdue
4th...Broncos
Player:_________________ Pts:_____

1st...Payton's blocker
2nd...#26
3rd...4-Year Penn St. starter
4th...1980 rookie
Player:_________________ Pts:_____

1st...1982 Yankees selection
2nd...1986 Buccs selection
3rd... Vincent Edward
4th... "He Knows"
Player:_________________ Pts:_____

1st...1993 Padres draftee
2nd...Huskie
3rd...Retired a Patriot
4th...Bengals
Player:_________________ Pts:_____

1st...Early 90's Gator star
2nd...1000 yard rookie
3rd...Browns
4th...Buccaneers drafted
Player:_________________ Pts:_____

1st...1st Round 1989
2nd...Bulldog star
3rd...#38
4th...Steelers
Player:_________________ Pts:_____

31

1st…8 straight 1000 yard years
2nd…Retired a Dolphin
3rd…#34
4th…Longtime Bill
Player:_________________ Pts:_____

32

1st…1999 Cavalier
2nd…2000 Cardinal
3rd…2003 Buccaneers
4th…2004 Bears
Player:_________________ Pts:_____

33

1st…Two 14-TD seasons
2nd…258 Lb. Buckeye
3rd…Bengal bruiser
4th…1984 Dolphin
Player:_________________ Pts:_____

34

1st…Chiefs rookie
2nd…1000 yard rookie
3rd…1981 rookie
4th…#2 Pick rookie
Player:_________________ Pts:_____

35

1st…2003 Auburn 1000 yarder
2nd…2004 Auburn 1000 yarder
3rd…2005 5th overall pick
4th…Fancy car nickname
Player:_________________ Pts:_____

36

1st…NCAA 2000 yarder
2nd…NCAA All-Time rusher
3rd…NCAA Heisman winner
4th…258 Lb. Giant
Player:_________________ Pts:_____

1st…"He Hate Me"
2nd…XFL Outlaws
3rd…Not dumb
4th…Western Kentucky
Player:________________ Pts:_____

1st…1973 1000 yarder
2nd…1974 1000 yarder
3rd…Colorado ST. 1000 yarder
4th…Rams
Player:________________ Pts:_____

1st…Synonym for holy man
2nd…Non-Drafted Raven
3rd…TD machine
4th…Chiefs
Player:________________ Pts:_____

1st…Razorback fullback
2nd…1990 pick
3rd…1690 yards 1992
4th…5 year Steeler
Player:________________ Pts:_____

1st…2668 career U of Georgia yards
2nd…1990 #1 Pick
3rd…1990's Giant
4th…5x 1000 yarder
Player:________________ Pts:_____

1st…"Not Todd or Kerry"
2nd…1983 1000 yarder
3rd…1990 Dolphin
4th…4647 career Patriot yards
Player:________________ Pts:_____

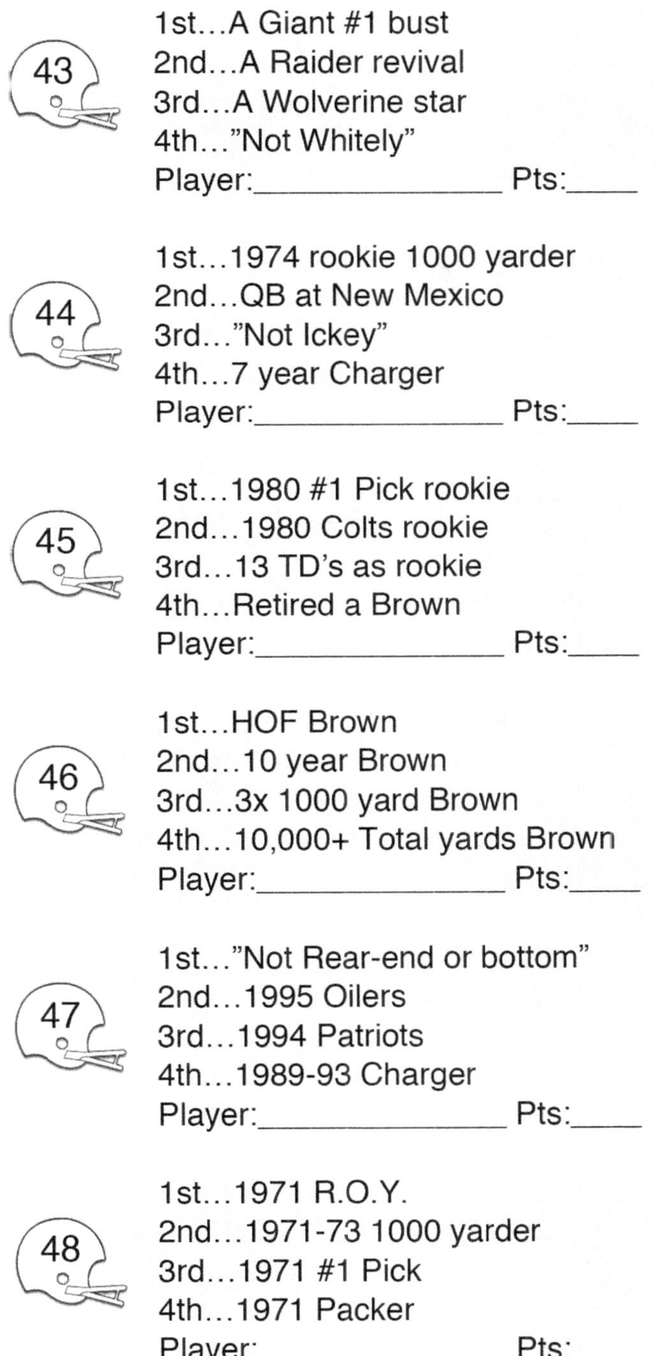

1st...A Giant #1 bust
2nd...A Raider revival
3rd...A Wolverine star
4th..."Not Whitely"
Player:_________________ Pts:_____

1st...1974 rookie 1000 yarder
2nd...QB at New Mexico
3rd..."Not Ickey"
4th...7 year Charger
Player:_________________ Pts:_____

1st...1980 #1 Pick rookie
2nd...1980 Colts rookie
3rd...13 TD's as rookie
4th...Retired a Brown
Player:_________________ Pts:_____

1st...HOF Brown
2nd...10 year Brown
3rd...3x 1000 yard Brown
4th...10,000+ Total yards Brown
Player:_________________ Pts:_____

1st..."Not Rear-end or bottom"
2nd...1995 Oilers
3rd...1994 Patriots
4th...1989-93 Charger
Player:_________________ Pts:_____

1st...1971 R.O.Y.
2nd...1971-73 1000 yarder
3rd...1971 #1 Pick
4th...1971 Packer
Player:_________________ Pts:_____

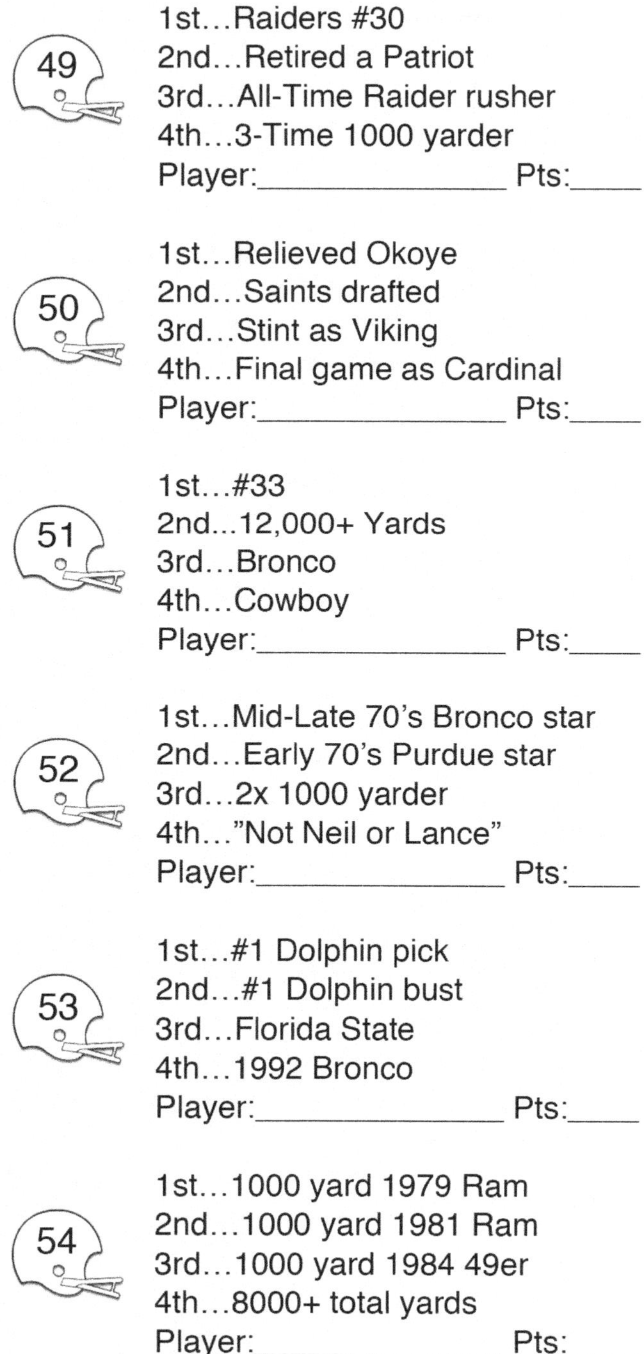

49
1st…Raiders #30
2nd…Retired a Patriot
3rd…All-Time Raider rusher
4th…3-Time 1000 yarder
Player:_________________ Pts:_____

50
1st…Relieved Okoye
2nd…Saints drafted
3rd…Stint as Viking
4th…Final game as Cardinal
Player:_________________ Pts:_____

51
1st…#33
2nd…12,000+ Yards
3rd…Bronco
4th…Cowboy
Player:_________________ Pts:_____

52
1st…Mid-Late 70's Bronco star
2nd…Early 70's Purdue star
3rd…2x 1000 yarder
4th…"Not Neil or Lance"
Player:_________________ Pts:_____

53
1st…#1 Dolphin pick
2nd…#1 Dolphin bust
3rd…Florida State
4th…1992 Bronco
Player:_________________ Pts:_____

54
1st…1000 yard 1979 Ram
2nd…1000 yard 1981 Ram
3rd…1000 yard 1984 49er
4th…8000+ total yards
Player:_________________ Pts:_____

55

1st…2004 Auburn phenomenon
2nd…2005 2nd overall pick
3rd…2006 1000 yarder
4th…Dolphins
Player:_________________ Pts:_____

56

1st…1st Redskin 1000 yard rookie
2nd…5'-8"
3rd…Started @ Notre Dame
4th…Finished @ Tampa Bay
Player:_________________ Pts:_____

57

1st…113 Games as Buccaneer
2nd…1 Game as Redskin 1990
3rd…15 Games as Lion 1990
4th…#32
Player:_________________ Pts:_____

58

1st…"Opposite of weak"
2nd…Tough fullback
3rd…2005 All-Pro
4th…13 year Seahawk
Player:_________________ Pts:_____

59

1st…1994 Seahawks draftee
2nd…Saints
3rd…Panthers
4th…1000 yard Dolphin
Player:_________________ Pts:_____

60

1st…1973 Heisman
2nd…Penn State
3rd…Chargers fullback
4th…Rams drafted
Player:_________________ Pts:_____

61

1st…1967 at Notre Dame
2nd…1968 at Pittsburgh
3rd…1969 at Vietnam
4th…1971 at Pittsburgh
Player:______________________ Pts:_____

62

1st…1000 yard Duck
2nd…1000 yard Bronco
3rd…1000 yard Brown
4th…72 yard Lion
Player:______________________ Pts:_____

63

1st…Bengals #28
2nd…South Carolina
3rd…1000+ yards 1992
4th…Retired a Falcon
Player:______________________ Pts:_____

64

1st…1st ever 1000 yard Colt
2nd…1974 record 72 receptions
3rd…Retired a Ram 1980
4th…Chargers
Player:______________________ Pts:_____

65

1st…Big bruising Brown
2nd…#33
3rd…10 year vet
4th…Michigan
Player:______________________ Pts:_____

66

1st…1000 yard 1976 49er
2nd…1000 yard 1978 Dolphin
3rd…5000+ career yards
4th…Kansas
Player:______________________ Pts:_____

67
1st...8 year Jet
2nd...Kutztown State
3rd...Undrafted
4th...(4X) 1000 yard kick-returner
Player:________________ Pts:_____

68
1st...Erric with (2) R's
2nd...Steelers
3rd...1993 1000 yarder
4th...1991 Falcon rookie
Player:________________ Pts:_____

69
1st...1974 R.O.Y.
2nd...1974 #1 Pick
3rd...1970's 49er
4th...1980's Redskin
Player:________________ Pts:_____

70
1st...827 RB receptions
2nd...101 receptions in 1995
3rd...Name means middle
4th...Longtime Cardinal
Player:________________ Pts:_____

71
1st...Steeler fullback
2nd...#33
3rd...Ran with Chiefs
4th..."Bam"
Player:________________ Pts:_____

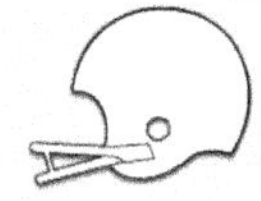 **EXTRA CREDIT** 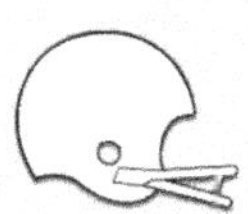

Extra Credit Questions are more challenging, therefore worth more points. Most of these players were in the league for only a short time, were low draftees, career back-ups, or just ranked in the unknown. But, they were all still pros. These are the answers that will make you a trivia pro.

Refer to the following point scale for all questions.
1st down...7 points
(Getting correct answer on first clue only)
2nd down...3 points
(Needing first two clues to get correct answer)
3rd down...2 points
(Needing first three clues to get correct anser)
4th down...1 point
(Needing all four clues to get correct answer)

72
1st...Packers 1988 pick
2nd...Texas A&M
3rd...59 receptions 1989
4th...Played every game 1988-91
Player:_________________ Pts:_____

73
1st...Ducks 1000 yard star
2nd...Not "Bam"
3rd...Shaun's relief
4th..."Mo"
Player:_________________ Pts:_____

74
1st...1978 1000 yard All-Pro
2nd...5 year Packer
3rd...2 year Buccaneer
4th...Memphis St.
Player:_________________ Pts:_____

75
1st…1981 rookie Chief
2nd…Career Chief
3rd…San Diego St.
4th…"Not Drew"
Player:________________ Pts:_____

76
1st…Pre Curt Warner
2nd…#47
3rd…6'-4"
4th…Seahawks original runner
Player:________________ Pts:_____

77
1st…1978 1000 yarder
2nd…1976 Colorado senior
3rd…1977 Chief rookie
4th…1981 Bronco bust
Player:________________ Pts:_____

78
1st…Beside Sweetness at Jackson State
2nd…1975 rookie
3rd…3 year Charger
4th…6 year Viking
Player:________________ Pts:_____

79
1st…"…and Fitch"
2nd…"Not Payton"
3rd…Retired an Eagle
4th…#1 Steeler pick
Player:________________ Pts:_____

80
1st…10 TD's rookie year
2nd…Chiefs #7 Pick
3rd…Class of 1981
4th…(2X) Alabama National Champ
Player:________________ Pts:_____

1st…5000+ yards at Nevada (Reno)
2nd…13 school records
3rd…Class of 1981
4th…7 year Raider
Player:_________________ Pts:_____

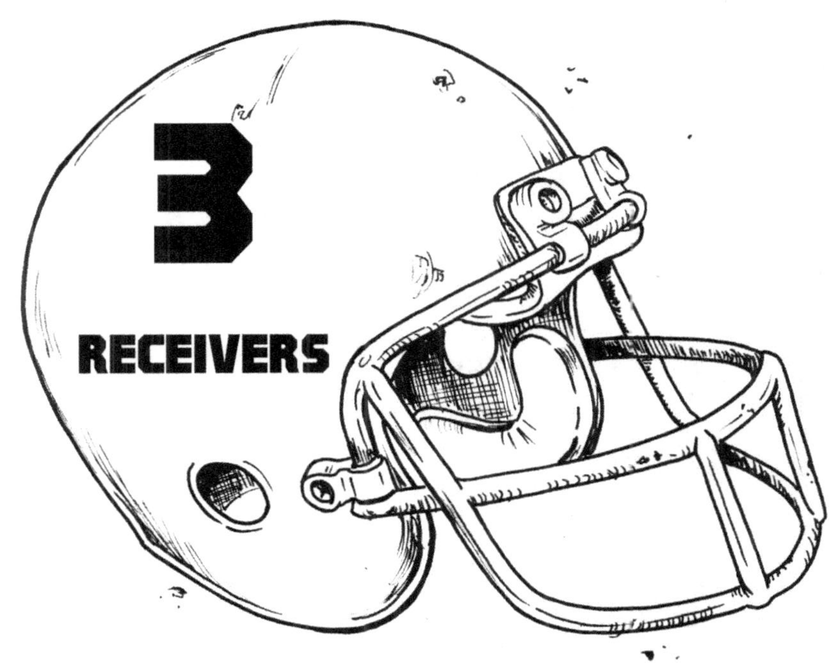

The most flamboyant position in football. The great ones must possess the speed of a cheetah and the balance of a ballerina.

Below you will find a blazing roster of receiver questions. Everyone from Hall of Famers to one game wonders, perfect catchers to over-the-top celebraters, top draftees to total busts.

Refer to the following point scale for all questions (except extra credit at chapter conclusion).

1st down...7 points

(Getting correct answer on first clue only)

2nd down...3 points

(Needing first two clues to get correct answer)

3rd down...2 points

(Needing first three clues to get correct anser)

4th down...1 point

(Needing all four clues to get correct answer)

1st...Cut by Chargers 2004
2nd...1000 kick-returner
3rd...Dolphins
4th...NCAA 8 punt-return TD's
Player:___________________ Pts:_____

1st...Argonauts
2nd...CFL
3rd...Notre Dame
4th..."Rocket"
Player:___________________ Pts:_____

1st...Gelatin
2nd...#1, 1996
3rd...Multi-1000 yarder
4th...Bills
Player:___________________ Pts:_____

1st...Career Dolphin
2nd...Career Gator
3rd...Career 8900+ yards
4th...#89
Player:___________________ Pts:_____

1st...Brother Butch NBA
2nd...Ohio State
3rd...Eagles waivers
4th...Vikings
Player:___________________ Pts:_____

1st...Team's first H.O.F'er
2nd...#80
3rd...Oilers drafted
4th...Career Seahawk
Player:___________________ Pts:_____

7

1st…"Stick-Em"
2nd…#25
3rd…Superbowl XI MVP
4th…1988 H.O.F. class
Player:_________________ Pts:_____

8

1st…WR, TE, RB, QB...
2nd…#11
3rd…Longtime Dolphin
4th…1981 draftee
Player:_________________ Pts:_____

9

1st…1990 H.O.F. inductee
2nd…All-Time TE
3rd…#82
4th…Browns
Player:_________________ Pts:_____

10

1st…336 yard record game
2nd…UCLA
3rd…Rams
4th…"Flipper"
Player:_________________ Pts:_____

11

1st…Part of the mouth
2nd…1984 R.O.Y.
3rd…#83
4th…Steelers
Player:_________________ Pts:_____

12

1st…"D-JAX"
2nd…Gator
3rd…Team records
4th…Seahawks
Player:_________________ Pts:_____

13

1st…Superbowl XX11 record
2nd…Patriots drafted
3rd…USFL Houston
4th…Redskins
Player:_________________ Pts:_____

14

1st…5 years CFL
2nd…1985 CFL MVP
3rd…"Swervyn"
4th…Raiders
Player:_________________ Pts:_____

15

1st…Jerry Rice counterpart
2nd…Punt-returner
3rd…Delaware State
4th…#82
Player:_________________ Pts:_____

16

1st…Not Andre
2nd…3rd round 1991
3rd…RB & WR @ Grambling
4th…Vikings
Player:_________________ Pts:_____

17

1st…"White Shoes"
2nd…Kick-returner
3rd…Oilers
4th…5'-9" Falcon
Player:_________________ Pts:_____

18

1st…Not Chris
2nd…USFL Star
3rd…Michigan
4th…Vikings
Player:_________________ Pts:_____

1st...#19 HOF
2nd...1962 rookie
3rd...Over 10,000 yards
4th...Chargers
Player:___________________ Pts:_____

1st...ACC record 3517 career yards
2nd...#1 Pick 2000
3rd...Seminole
4th...Seahawk punt-returner
Player:___________________ Pts:_____

1st...#1 Pick 1974
2nd...1976 1000 yarder
3rd...Colts
4th...Caucasian
Player:___________________ Pts:_____

1st...A brass musical instrument
2nd...Chiefs rookie
3rd...Memphis CFL 1995
4th...Saints records
Player:___________________ Pts:_____

1st...Religious name
2nd...Drafted by Bills
3rd...#1 Pick 1968
4th...Longtime Bronco
Player:___________________ Pts:_____

1st...& Tina Turner
2nd...Cardinals 1975 rookie
3rd...So. California WFL 1974
4th...Saints
Player:___________________ Pts:_____

25

1st…309 yard record game
2nd…10 Td's 1985
3rd…Not drafted
4th…Chiefs
Player:________________________ Pts:______

26

1st…Rookie record 90 receptions
2nd…7th player taken 1996
3rd…Ohio State
4th…Super Bowl star
Player:________________________ Pts:______

27

1st…A skin growth
2nd…Michigan
3rd…Class of 1996
4th…Giants
Player:________________________ Pts:______

28

1st…One of "3 Amigos"
2nd…Florida Gator
3rd…56 yard TD in Superbowl XXII
4th…#1 Pick 1987
Player:________________________ Pts:______

29

1st…Bobby Moore
2nd…University of Oregon
3rd…Cardinal #1 Pick 1972
4th…Married Felicia
Player:________________________ Pts:______

30

1st…"The Thrill"
2nd…1977 rookie
3rd…1000 yarder 1979-80
4th…Longtime Cowboy
Player:________________________ Pts:______

1st...1976 NFC R.O.Y.
2nd...#85
3rd...Vikings
4th...Multiple Pro-Bowls
Player:_________________ Pts:_____

1st...2000 Beaver
2nd...Initials
3rd...14 letters in last name
4th...Ocho Cinco's friend
Player:_________________ Pts:_____

1st...3rd overall pick 2005
2nd...2004 Belitnikoff Award
3rd...(3) 1000 yard NCAA seasons
4th...Wolverines
Player:_________________ Pts:_____

1st...1964 R.O.Y. receiver
2nd...Started out a RB
3rd...Redskins records
4th...Not Lawrence...
Player:_________________ Pts:_____

1st...WR of 1987 National Champs
2nd...Drafted by Saints
3rd...Lions
4th...Herman Moore's counterpart
Player:_________________ Pts:_____

1st...Rams drafted #12, 1979
2nd...Traded to Oilers 1985
3rd...Signed with Falcons 1992
4th...Multiple 1000 yard seasons
Player:_________________ Pts:_____

37

1st...1974 rookie Steeler
2nd...1979, 1000+ yards
3rd...1981, 1000+ yards
4th...1984, 1000+ yards
Player:_______________________ Pts:______

38

1st...Fastest WR in 1988 Draft
2nd...Chargers #1 Pick
3rd...4-Time Charger Pro-Bowler
4th...Broncos
Player:_______________________ Pts:______

39

1st...Undefeated 1972
2nd...Ohio State
3rd...A battle ground
4th...Dolphins star
Player:_______________________ Pts:______

40

1st...Wrestler SGT. _______
2nd...Dictionary company
3rd...San Diego State
4th...1986 Browns rookie
Player:_______________________ Pts:______

41

1st...James Lofton tandem
2nd...#1 Pick 1978
3rd...Lambeau speedster
4th...Goggle glasses
Player:_______________________ Pts:______

42

1st...Dolphins #1 Pick 1993
2nd...Not "The Juice"
3rd...(2) rookie punt-return TD's
4th...Penn State
Player:_______________________ Pts:______

1st...A tree limb
2nd...#21
3rd...Raider for over a decade
4th...Over 60 TD's
Player:________________ Pts:_____

1st...1000 yard 1986 rookie
2nd...Louisville
3rd...#81
4th...Consistent Oiler
Player:________________ Pts:_____

1st...1000 yard 1986 rookie
2nd...Boston University
3rd...#80
4th...Consistent Colt
Player:________________ Pts:_____

1st...Big play Jet
2nd...1977 rookie
3rd...12 TD 1986 leader
4th...Double W's
Player:________________ Pts:_____

1st...Synonym for home
2nd...1980 rookie
3rd...Team's early All-Time yards leader
4th...Buccaneers
Player:________________ Pts:_____

1st...1st Syracuse 1000 yarder
2nd...1990 rookie
3rd...#85
4th...Jets #1 Pick
Player:________________ Pts:_____

49

1st... 2006 ACC P.O.Y.
2nd...2006 Belitnikoff Award
3rd...2006 Yellow Jackets
4th...2007 2nd overall pick
Player:__________________ Pts:_____

50

1st...Rice QB, drafted as WR
2nd...1994 rookie
3rd... "...and Ernie"
4th...Falcons
Player:__________________ Pts:_____

51

1st...Not a TV Munster
2nd...6'-3" Virginian
3rd...Perriman counterpart
4th...Lions
Player:__________________ Pts:_____

52

1st...Broncos #80
2nd...1995 rookie Broncos #80
3rd...Superbowl Broncos #80
4th...Decade+ Broncos #80
Player:__________________ Pts:_____

53

1st...1st ever Texan Pro-Bowler
2nd...3rd overall 2003 Pick
3rd...Hurricanes
4th...#80
Player:__________________ Pts:_____

54

1st...Synonym for jacket
2nd...1000 yard TE
3rd...TE record 96 receptions
4th...Longtime Patriot
Player:__________________ Pts:_____

55

1st...Inaugural Jaguar
2nd...Cowboys drafted
3rd...(7) consecutive 1000 yarders
4th...Not Keenan
Player:_________________ Pts:_____

56

1st...QB @ Arkansas
2nd...Davey's locker
3rd...#1 Pick, 2005
4th...6'-6", 242 Lbs.
Player:_________________ Pts:_____

57

1st...Stanford 1990
2nd...Giants drafted
3rd...49ers
4th...Broncos #87
Player:_________________ Pts:_____

58

1st...Caught Peyton's record 49th TD
2nd...Superbowl XXXV TD
3rd...Ravens pick
4th...Colts 1000 yarder
Player:_________________ Pts:_____

59

1st...Bengals, #81
2nd...#1 Pick
3rd...U of Miami
4th...1985 All-Rookie Team
Player:_________________ Pts:_____

60

1st...1972 Heisman
2nd...Four years CFL
3rd...Cornhusker
4th...Chargers #1 Pick
Player:_________________ Pts:_____

61

1st…Jaguars
2nd…Redskins
3rd…Browns
4th…Buccaneers & Chargers
Player:_________________ Pts:_____

62

1st…#1 Pick LSU
2nd…Rams
3rd…Saints
4th…Bears
Player:_________________ Pts:_____

63

1st…1980 NFL Man of the Year
2nd…Tallest 70's WR
3rd…Over 8000 career yards
4th…Longtime Eagle
Player:_________________ Pts:_____

64

1st…1000 Yard Favre fave
2nd…#86
3rd…Virginia Tech
4th…Class of 1995
Player:_________________ Pts:_____

65

1st…Rice counterpart
2nd…#1 Pick
3rd…Class of 1995
4th…Initials
Player:_________________ Pts:_____

66

1st…1996 College National Champ
2nd…Gators
3rd…5'-8" speedster
4th…Buccaneers
Player:_________________ Pts:_____

67

1st…Caught Favre's 400th TD
2nd…2007 rookie
3rd…#85
4th…Packers pick
Player:_____________________ Pts:______

68

1st…Buccaneers TE
2nd…Played baseball in 1976
3rd…Drafted by Oilers
4th…4 Pro-Bowls
Player:_____________________ Pts:______

69

1st…RB,WR,KR,QB @USC
2nd…Da Bears
3rd…1993 rookie
4th…"Not Tim"
Player:_____________________ Pts:______

70

1st…Bengals #1 Pick
2nd…1000 yard rookie KR
3rd…Tennessee
4th…"Not Tony or Willie"
Player:_____________________ Pts:______

71

1st…"Super"
2nd…#85
3rd…Dolphins
4th…Half of "Marks Brothers"
Player:_____________________ Pts:______

 **EXTRA CREDIT** 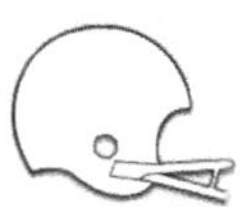

Extra Credit Questions are more challenging, therefore worth more points. Most of these players were in the league for only a short time, were low draftees, career back-ups, or just ranked in the unknown. But, they were all still pros. These are the answers that will make you a trivia pro.

Refer to the following point scale for all questions.
1st down...7 points
(Getting correct answer on first clue only)
2nd down...3 points
(Needing first two clues to get correct answer)
3rd down...2 points
(Needing first three clues to get correct anser)
4th down...1 point
(Needing all four clues to get correct answer)

72
1st...1000 yard Tight End
2nd...One year wonder
3rd...1981 All-Pro
4th...Career Viking
Player:_________________ Pts:_____

73
1st...Bengals #1 pick
2nd...Class of 1976
3rd..."Not James"
4th...Oklahoma star
Player:_________________ Pts:_____

74
1st...American explorers namesake
2nd...Round #10, 1987
3rd...Mississippi State
4th...6 year Seahawk
Player:_________________ Pts:_____

1st…Shares hip-hopper name
2nd…1985 rookie
3rd…1986 retiree
4th…Vikings
Player:_________________ Pts:_____

1st…1992 Hurricane
2nd…4th Round Pick
3rd…4 Year Buccaneer
4th…Not spelled "Horse"
Player:_________________ Pts:_____

1st…Dolphins #81
2nd…Dolphins rookie 1978
3rd…Dolphins 7 year vet
4th…Penn St. alumni
Player:_________________ Pts:_____

1st…Dolphins #81
2nd…Dolphins rookie 1966
3rd…Dolphins 12 year vet
4th…Nations leading scorer at Tulsa
Player:_________________ Pts:_____

1st…"Bigger than a pond"
2nd…Notre Dame
3rd…1994 Pick
4th…4 year Chief
Player:_________________ Pts:_____

1st…Oilers 1980 rookie
2nd…1st 3 years Special Teams
3rd…Next 2 years 1000+ yards
4th…All 7 years as Oiler
Player:_________________ Pts:_____

1st…9 year Bear WR
2nd…Started out a cornerback
3rd…Class of 1976
4th…#84
Player:_________________ Pts:_____

1st…Falcons 1991 top pick
2nd…Colorado star
3rd…Bronco
4th…Seahawk
Player:_________________ Pts:_____

1st…Not fried, white or jasmine
2nd…Retired a Seahawk
3rd…Viking deep threat
4th…1000-yard WR
Player:_________________ Pts:_____

1st…1973 Cowboy undrafted free agent
2nd…Was QB at Tulsa
3rd…1000-yard WR
4th…Drawing past tense
Player:_________________ Pts:_____

1st…Lifetime Steeler WR
2nd…League leading 12 TD's 2002
3rd…All-time team reception leader
4th…Ketchup brand
Player:_________________ Pts:_____

1st…Short 5'-8" Oiler
2nd…1980 rookie from Texas A&M
3rd…All-Rookie Team kick returner
4th…Needs no bug spray
Player:_________________ Pts:_____

The most uncelebrated positions in football. From the giants up front taking on two blockers to the intercepters in back taking picks to the house, these guys are the oil in the team machine.

Below you will find a crushing roster of defensive questions. Everyone from Hall of Famers to one game wonders, head-hunting safeties to QB sacking linebackers, and all the work horses in between.

Refer to the following point scale for all questions (except extra credit at chapter conclusion).

1st down...7 points
(Getting correct answer on first clue only)
2nd down...3 points
(Needing first two clues to get correct answer)
3rd down...2 points
(Needing first three clues to get correct anser)
4th down...1 point
(Needing all four clues to get correct answer)

1st...2004 Defensive R.O.Y.
2nd...#1 Pick 2002
3rd...Not Jake
4th...Record 358 INT yards
Player:________________ Pts:_____

1st...#72
2nd...350 Lbs.
3rd...DT & RB
4th..."Fridge"
Player:________________ Pts:_____

1st...Longtime Browns CB
2nd...1983-84 USFL
3rd...5'-9"
4th...Louisville
Player:________________ Pts:_____

1st...Name of wizard
2nd...Television series regular
3rd...Rams
4th...#1 Pick 1962
Player:________________ Pts:_____

1st...Old soda commercial
2nd...1972 Defensive MVP
3rd..."Mean"
4th...Steelers
Player:________________ Pts:_____

1st...17 rookie sacks
2nd...#99
3rd...6'-5" DE
4th...Jets
Player:________________ Pts:_____

7

1st…Buccaneers 1981 #1 Pick
2nd…151 rookie tackles
3rd…Pitt.
4th…Last name a color
Player:_______________ Pts:_____

8

1st…1999 Butkis Award
2nd…2001-03 NFC Pro-Bowler
3rd…Penn State
4th…Redskins
Player:_______________ Pts:_____

9

1st…Class of 1990 H.O.F.
2nd…6'-7" linebacker
3rd…4 Superbowls
4th…Raiders
Player:_______________ Pts:_____

10

1st…Titans #1 Pick
2nd…14 1/2 rookie sacks
3rd…1999 Defensive R.O.Y.
4th…"The Freak"
Player:_______________ Pts:_____

11

1st…St. Louis Cardinals
2nd…Atlanta Braves
3rd…Atlanta Falcons
4th…Safety / Outfielder
Player:_______________ Pts:_____

12

1st…Powder for skiing
2nd…1989 Lombardi Award
3rd…Chiefs #1 Pick
4th…Michigan State
Player:_______________ Pts:_____

13

1st…Small red fruit
2nd…Longtime Chief
3rd…A non-drafted star safety
4th…#20
Player:_________________ Pts:_____

14

1st…Linebacker, not Derrick
2nd…Mike Singletary's nephew
3rd…1989 #1 Pick
4th…Buccaneers
Player:_________________ Pts:_____

15

1st…"Neon"
2nd…"Prime Time"
3rd…#21
4th…Outfielder, KR, PR, WR, CB
Player:_________________ Pts:_____

16

1st…All-Time great #26
2nd…Purdue speedster
3rd…NFL Network
4th…Steelers
Player:_________________ Pts:_____

17

1st…Intense Eyes
2nd…#50
3rd…Superstar LB
4th…Superbowl Bear
Player:_________________ Pts:_____

18

1st…Steelers #1 Pick 1975
2nd…Seahawks "Ring Of Honor"
3rd…Cornerback
4th…Deceased
Player:_________________ Pts:_____

19

1st…A Bird with Talons
2nd…2005 Lombardi Trophy
3rd…2006 5th overall pick
4th…Initials
Player:________________ Pts:_____

20

1st…Seahawks DE / LB
2nd…1987 Rookie
3rd…#1 Pick
4th…"Not Tiger"
Player:________________ Pts:_____

21

1st…1980 rookie CB
2nd…10 year Ram
3rd…"Not Michael"
4th…Lions
Player:________________ Pts:_____

22

1st…2nd overall pick 1987
2nd…Colts
3rd…Falcons
4th…Bills
Player:________________ Pts:_____

23

1st…13 year Patriot
2nd…Cornerback
3rd…#1 Pick 1977
4th…"Everybody Loves…"
Player:________________ Pts:_____

24

1st…1999 Defensive R.O.Y.
2nd…#99
3rd…Hurricanes
4th…"From a tree"
Player:________________ Pts:_____

25
1st…Braves minor-leaguer
2nd…Seminole star
3rd…Packers pick
4th…"T. Bucket"
Player:________________ Pts:_____

26
1st…Bigger than a pond
2nd…1989 rookie safety
3rd…Bruins
4th…Steelers
Player:________________ Pts:_____

27
1st…Name of a beer
2nd…Seahawks top pick
3rd…285 Lb. DT
4th…1994 All-Rookie Team
Player:________________ Pts:_____

28
1st…Indians drafted as pitcher
2nd…Tigers drafted as outfielder
3rd…Patriots drafted as safety
4th…Huskies played him at rover
Player:________________ Pts:_____

29
1st…12 year Bear
2nd…#45
3rd…Drafted by Dolphins
4th…All-Pro safety
Player:________________ Pts:_____

30
1st…"New York Sack Exchange"
2nd…#93
3rd…1978 National Champ Alabama
4th…11 Year Jet
Player:________________ Pts:_____

1st...#54
2nd...5'-11' linebacker
3rd...Texas Tech
4th...Dolphin middle mainstay
Player:_________________ Pts:_____

1st...6'-4" CB with glasses
2nd...Eagles 1973 Pick
3rd..."A fragrant shrub"
4th...Redskin Pro-Bowler
Player:_________________ Pts:_____

1st...All-American Notre Dame DE
2nd...Lombardi Trophy
3rd...Outland Trophy
4th...1978 Bengals #1 Pick
Player:_________________ Pts:_____

1st...Long blonde hair
2nd...1985 Ram rookie
3rd...15 year LB-DE
4th...Steelers
Player:_________________ Pts:_____

1st...Chargers sack specialist
2nd...1975 #1 Pick
3rd...Retired a 49er
4th...DT
Player:_________________ Pts:_____

1st...Ohio State LB
2nd...2 Year Buffalo LB
3rd...8 Year Lions LB
4th...1988 Rookie LB
Player:_________________ Pts:_____

1st...Tall neck pad
2nd...#51
3rd...Perennial Pro-Bowler
4th...Dolphin MLB
Player:________________ Pts:_____

1st...1977 SEC P.O.Y.
2nd...1978 #1 Pick
3rd...1979,80,82,84,86 All-Pro
4th...Chiefs
Player:________________ Pts:_____

1st...Cousin a baseball Giants SS
2nd...9 Year LB
3rd...9 Year Eagle
4th...Class of 1974
Player:________________ Pts:_____

1st...3 Defensive TD's 1995
2nd...1990's Cardinal corner
3rd...Interception machine
4th...4 year Ram corner
Player:________________ Pts:_____

1st...#97 DT
2nd...Notre Dame
3rd...Retired a Redskin
4th...Da Bears
Player:________________ Pts:_____

1st...10 year 49er DE
2nd...1976 All-Pro
3rd...Had heart
4th...Morris Brown College
Player:________________ Pts:_____

1st...Seahawks #1 Pick
2nd...Career Seahawk
3rd...A Hurricane
4th...#96 H.O.F.
Player:_________________ Pts:_____

1st...19 year linebacker
2nd...4 year Pro-Bowler
3rd...3 year Falcon
4th...16 year Brown
Player:_________________ Pts:_____

1st...1973 R.O.Y.
2nd...#1 Pick
3rd...Defensive tackle
4th...Bears All-Pro
Player:_________________ Pts:_____

1st...13 Year 49er DT
2nd...1994 #1 Pick
3rd..."Not Steve"
4th...Notre Dame
Player:_________________ Pts:_____

1st...20 1/2 sacks in 1981
2nd...Temple
3rd...Played DT, NT, DE
4th...Jets
Player:_________________ Pts:_____

1st...Lifetime Viking
2nd...6 consecutive Pro-Bowls
3rd...6'-5" linebacker
4th...Class of 1974
Player:_________________ Pts:_____

49

1st…Lifetime Oiler
2nd…8 consecutive All-Pros
3rd…#1 Pick LB
4th…Class of 1975
Player:_________________ Pts:_____

50

1st…1994 rookie CB
2nd…Texas A&M
3rd…#1 Pick
4th…Only Pro-Bowl Jet CB
Player:_________________ Pts:_____

51

1st…Syracuse LB
2nd…#53
3rd…2000 #1 Pick
4th…8 year Titan tackler
Player:_________________ Pts:_____

52

1st…2008 H.O.F. selection
2nd…Defensive lineman
3rd…Charger Pro-Bowler
4th…Superbowl 49er
Player:_________________ Pts:_____

53

1st…5th overall pick 2003
2nd…Cornerback
3rd…Kansas State sprinter
4th…Cowboys
Player:_________________ Pts:_____

54

1st…Super Bowl XX MVP
2nd…Tennessee star DE
3rd…17 sacks in 1985
4th…"Scratch and …."
Player:_________________ Pts:_____

5
FOOTBALL FAMILIES

The transference of athletic DNA skills is a more common occurance than one might think in professional football. Manning QB's pass it down generations and Matthew's defenders multiply with the passing years.

Below you will find a bonding roster of football family questions. Everyone from sibling rivalries to father-son lineages.

Refer to the following point scale for all questions (except extra credit at chapter conclusion).

1st down...7 points
(Getting correct answer on first clue only)
2nd down...3 points
(Needing first two clues to get correct answer)
3rd down...2 points
(Needing first three clues to get correct anser)
4th down...1 point
(Needing all four clues to get correct answer)

1st…Both @ USC
2nd…Seahawk son
3rd…1978 rookie
4th…Patriot
Player:_________________ Pts:_____

1st…Father old 49er
2nd…Son Chiefs
3rd…4000+ yards 1983
4th…QB
Player:_________________ Pts:_____

1st…Born into QB
2nd…Texas Longhorns
3rd…Hospitalized during game
4th…Father a Giant
Player:_________________ Pts:_____

1st…Browns #1 Pick
2nd…RB & KR
3rd…Dad Terry a RB too
4th…Texas star
Player:_________________ Pts:_____

1st…Brother Earl Cardinals WR
2nd…Drafted 1975
3rd…RB
4th…Redskin rookie
Player:_________________ Pts:_____

1st…1993 Rookie
2nd…Both played WR
3rd…Vikings
4th…Brother is a Rocket
Player:_________________ Pts:_____

1st…Father a Browns WR
2nd…Son a WR
3rd…TCU
4th…Oilers
Family Name:________________ Pts:_____

1st…Silver
2nd…#84
3rd…Career ending injury
4th…Brother a Bronco
Player:________________ Pts:_____

1st…BBQ restaurant chain
2nd…Oklahoma
3rd…Brother on same team
4th…Buccaneers
Player:________________ Pts:_____

1st…Had 2 QB sons
2nd…1977 rookie
3rd…TE
4th…Patriots
Player:________________ Pts:_____

1st…5'-7" Giant
2nd…21 TD's in 1985
3rd…Brother Jamie
4th…#20
Player:________________ Pts:_____

1st…After Largent
2nd…Brother a Lion
3rd…Sharp Hurricanes
4th…#89
Player:________________ Pts:_____

13

1st...Brother 1000 yarders
2nd...Brother running-backs
3rd...Brother Browns
4th...Brother teammates
Family Name:_________________ Pts:_____

14

1st...Perfect season
2nd...Both QB's
3rd...Son a Bronco
4th...Dad a Dolphin
Family Name:_________________ Pts:_____

15

1st...1975 Heisman runner-up
2nd...Wore glasses
3rd...NFL brother George
4th...NFL brother Nelson
Player:_________________ Pts:_____

16

1st...H.O.F. father
2nd...Both TE's
3rd...Son Browns
4th...Dad Chargers
Family Name:_________________ Pts:_____

17

1st...Bald brothers
2nd...Pro-Bowl brothers
3rd...One a RB
4th...One a CB
Family Name:_________________ Pts:_____

18

1st...Both on 1970's Buccs
2nd...Dad a coach
3rd...WR
4th...USC
Family Name:_________________ Pts:_____

19

1st…Jonathan
2nd…Jordan
3rd…Brothers
4th…Defense
Family Name:________________ Pts:_____

20

1st…Ted Sr. All-Pro 1944-46
2nd…Ted Jr. Redskin center
3rd…Ted Sr. Packers RB
4th…Ted Jr. a Falcon
Family Name:________________ Pts:_____

21

1st…U of Colorado bro's
2nd…Both offensive linemen
3rd…Both from Oregon
4th…Both #1 Picks
Family Name:________________ Pts:_____

22

1st…Cornerback brothers
2nd…San Diego St. brothers
3rd…17 combined NFL years
4th…Jackson brothers
Family Name:________________ Pts:_____

23

1st…Son won 1994 Heisman
2nd…Father Teddy RB for 1963 Bengals
3rd…Son a rookie 1000 yard RB
4th…Son a quick Bear bust
Family Name:________________ Pts:_____

24

1st…Father played at Louisville
2nd…Brother played at Louisville
3rd…He played at Louisville
4th…Drafted by Packers
Player:________________ Pts:_____

25
1st...Twin offensive linemen
2nd...One a Redskins guard
3rd...Other a Rams center
4th...Both attended Michigan St.
Family Name:_________________ Pts:_____

26
1st...Dad a Jets RB
2nd...Son a Cowboys RB
3rd...Same name (son a Jr.)
4th...Both Golden Gophers
Family Name:_________________ Pts:_____

27
1st...LSU receivers
2nd...21 combined years
3rd...Brian
4th...Todd
Family Name:_________________ Pts:_____

28
1st...Both Raiders
2nd...Both Trojans
3rd...Dad Marv 1965 rookie
4th...Son a #1 Pick bust
Family Name:_________________ Pts:_____

29
1st...Father Ron a RB
2nd...Both Buckeyes
3rd...Son a 1st Round Pick
4th...Son Shawn a CB
Family Name:_________________ Pts:_____

30
1st...Young QB bro's
2nd...One a Cardinals Pick
3rd...One a Browns Pick
4th...Josh & Luke
Family Name:_________________ Pts:_____

31

1st…"Not Fig…"
2nd…Brother a Viking
3rd…Brother a Cowboy
4th…Both played in 1980's-90's
Family Name:_________________ Pts:_____

32

1st…1997 rookie brothers
2nd…Both 2nd round picks
3rd…One a Packer safety
4th…One a Raven linebacker
Family Name:_________________ Pts:_____

33

1st…Mike QB on 1987 Bucs
2nd…David WR on 1981 Colts
3rd…Son Bengals head coach
4th…Father a H.O.F. coach
Family Name:_________________ Pts:_____

34

1st…TE brothers
2nd…Older a 1981 Seahawks pick
3rd…Younger a 1983 Saints pick
4th…Older a Vikings coach
Family Name:_________________ Pts:_____

35

1st…Kicker brothers
2nd…Joaquin a 1983 rookie
3rd…Max a 1986 rookie
4th…Luis a 1987 rookie
Family Name:_________________ Pts:_____

36

1st…Linebacker lineage
2nd…Casey a Duck
3rd…Father & Grandfather were Browns
4th…Packers backer
Family Name:_________________ Pts:_____

6
I PICKS

    The first pick in the college draft is always a gamble. Whether teams are looking for a career blocker to protect their star QB's blindside or an immediate impact skilled position to fill a free agency hole, any pick can be a crapshoot.

    Below you will find a risky roster of #1 draft picks. Some were college stars that turned in to pro washouts, and others were iffy choices that took their team to glory.

    Refer to the following point scale for all questions (except extra credit at chapter conclusion).

1st down...7 points
(Getting correct answer on first clue only)
2nd down...3 points
(Needing first two clues to get correct answer)
3rd down...2 points
(Needing first three clues to get correct anser)
4th down...1 point
(Needing all four clues to get correct answer)

1st...Grogan's successor
2nd...Illinois
3rd...#11
4th...Patriots
Player:_________________ Pts:_____

1st...1989 WR
2nd...Uses middle name too
3rd...Oklahoma State
4th...Patriots
Player:_________________ Pts:_____

1st...#19
2nd...1st Pick of 1996
3rd...Trojan ball boy
4th...Jets
Player:_________________ Pts:_____

1st...1990 RB
2nd...Penn State star
3rd...Senior Bowl MVP
4th...Jets flop
Player:_________________ Pts:_____

1st...Texas A&M safety
2nd...1993 rookie
3rd...Raiders
4th..."Psycho" motel name
Player:_________________ Pts:_____

1st...Led nation in TD's 1992
2nd...Bulldog
3rd...Cardinals pick
4th...Injured 49er
Player:_________________ Pts:_____

7

1st...1984 Outland Trophy
2nd...#78
3rd...DE
4th...Bills sack machine
Player:_________________ Pts:_____

8

1st...Girlfriend burned mansion
2nd...Colts drafted
3rd..."Bad Moon"
4th...Falcons star
Player:_________________ Pts:_____

9

1st...2006 cornerback pick
2nd...Clemson track star
3rd...Rams
4th..."____" your shoe!
Player:_________________ Pts:_____

10

1st...1986 QB
2nd...Iowa
3rd...A Big 10 All-Time leader
4th...Not long for the league
Player:_________________ Pts:_____

11

1st...1990 49ers pick
2nd...RB / KR
3rd...5'-8" speedster
4th...Seminoles
Player:_________________ Pts:_____

12

1st...Redskins QB
2nd...Tennessee's All-Time records
3rd...Class of 1994 Draft
4th...Candy bar
Player:_________________ Pts:_____

13
1st…Mets minor leagues
2nd…Penn State
3rd…RB
4th…Vikings
Player:________________ Pts:_____

14
1st…Gators fullback
2nd…Uses middle initial
3rd…Steelers
4th…Seahawks
Player:________________ Pts:_____

15
1st…XFL
2nd…QB
3rd…Virginia Tech hero
4th…49er Flop
Player:________________ Pts:_____

16
1st…1986 fullback
2nd…Ohio State
3rd…Dolphins
4th…Eagles
Player:________________ Pts:_____

17
1st…Big Dolphins safety
2nd…25th Pick 1989
3rd…Florida Gators
4th…Longtime starter
Player:________________ Pts:_____

18
1st…Rams #1 mistake
2nd…1995 Cornhusker
3rd…First RB picked in draft
4th…#21
Player:________________ Pts:_____

19
1st…Jets 1000 yarder
2nd…An animated show
3rd…1985 rookie WR
4th…Jets
Player:_________________ Pts:_____

20
1st…1989 Cardinals
2nd…QB
3rd…Washington State
4th…Not Sebastian…
Player:_________________ Pts:_____

21
1st…Dolphin blonde LB
2nd…Class of 1977
3rd…LSU
4th…Initials for name
Player:_________________ Pts:_____

22
1st…Led nation @ Rice
2nd…1977 rookie
3rd…Vikings QB
4th…Seinfeld character
Player:_________________ Pts:_____

23
1st…1990 Falcons pick
2nd…RB / KR
3rd…Pac-10
4th…5'-7"
Player:_________________ Pts:_____

24
1st…Blocked for Neal Anderson
2nd…Stanford
3rd…232 Lb. fullback
4th…Not mustard
Player:_________________ Pts:_____

1st…1981 Seahawk
2nd…UCLA
3rd…Pro-Bowl safety
4th… "…Does It."
Player:_________________ Pts:_____

1st…1974 Oregon Duck
2nd…Drafted by football's Patriots
3rd…Drafted by baseball's Royals
4th…Tight End
Player:_________________ Pts:_____

1st…Broke F. Tarkenton's records
2nd…Broke Y.A. Tittle's records
3rd…Broke Into League in 1979
4th…Broke into TV job after career
Player:_________________ Pts:_____

1st…2002 Heisman
2nd…#9
3rd…Trojan
4th…Throws to #85
Player:_________________ Pts:_____

1st…6'-9" DE
2nd…#72
3rd…Cowboys
4th…"Too Tall"
Player:_________________ Pts:_____

1st…2004 WR
2nd…1000 yard rookie
3rd…Louisiana St.
4th…Buccaneer
Player:_________________ Pts:_____

1st...NFL reception leader 1980-82
2nd...TE
3rd...#80
4th...Chargers
Player:___________________ Pts:_____

1st...Peyton target
2nd...U of Miami
3rd...Class of 2001
4th...Colts
Player:___________________ Pts:_____

1st...Over a decade with Oilers
2nd...WR
3rd...1970 rookie
4th...Set team records
Player:___________________ Pts:_____

1st...1980 All-Rookie Team WR
2nd...Peaceful man in robe
3rd...#81
4th...Longtime Redskins
Player:___________________ Pts:_____

1st...1993 DT
2nd...All-American @ Alabama
3rd...Bengals
4th...Much better as collegian
Player:___________________ Pts:_____

1st...Cardinals #1 1979
2nd...Hurricanes
3rd...1000 yards in 12th year
4th...A Parcels RB
Player:___________________ Pts:_____

1st...Bills 1984 pick
2nd...Rookie 1000 yarder
3rd...Notre Dame alumni
4th...Rams 1000 yarder
Player:___________________ Pts:_____

1st...Buccaneers 1979 Team MVP
2nd...USC RB
3rd...Played high school with Chet Lemon
4th...Song title "Hells-_____"
Player:___________________ Pts:_____

1st...Seahawks 1980 choice
2nd...Rewrote Seattle records
3rd...DE
4th...Color of money
Player:___________________ Pts:_____

1st...8 year Bronco
2nd...Over 4000 yards
3rd...(2) 1000 yard years
4th...Purdue stud
Player:___________________ Pts:_____

1st...Eagles 1993 pick
2nd...Defensive Tackle
3rd...Colorado
4th..."Not Nemoy"
Player:___________________ Pts:_____

1st...1976 premiere CB
2nd...A.S.U.
3rd...8-Time All-Pro
4th...Patriots
Player:___________________ Pts:_____

43

1st…"Hacksaw"
2nd…Rams Class of '70
3rd…15 year vet
4th…49ers
Player:_______________ Pts:_____

44

1st…Alabama CB
2nd…1993 draft
3rd…Packers pick
4th…Cowboys
Player:_______________ Pts:_____

45

1st…1st overall 1993
2nd…Before Mirer
3rd…Before Brady
4th…Washington State
Player:_______________ Pts:_____

46

1st…New Cowboy corner
2nd…5th overall pick 2003
3rd…Kansas St.
4th…R.O.Y. runner-up
Player:_______________ Pts:_____

47

1st…Record 102 TE Receptions
2nd…Led All NCAA TE 1996
3rd…Class of 1997
4th…Mr. Chiefs
Player:_______________ Pts:_____

48

1st…Packers Smith
2nd…Running Back
3rd…1974 pick
4th…Richmond
Player:_______________ Pts:_____

1st…Packers Smith
2nd…Wide Receiver
3rd…1973 pick
4th…Florida St.
Player:_______________________ Pts:______

1st…Falcons #56
2nd…Rookie 1998
3rd…Punishing LB
4th…Georgia Tech
Player:_______________________ Pts:______

1st…Nigerian
2nd…Chiefs #1 DE
3rd…Class of 2006
4th…Penn State
Player:_______________________ Pts:______

1st…"Not Dynamite"
2nd…Huskies
3rd…1995 RB pick
4th…Raiders
Player:_______________________ Pts:______

1st…1st RB taken 1982
2nd…#20
3rd…Stanford
4th…Vikings
Player:_______________________ Pts:______

1st…Patriots #55
2nd…Linebacker
3rd…2-Time All Pac-10
4th…1990 rookie
Player:_______________________ Pts:______

55

1st…LSU native
2nd…#7
3rd…1973 rookie
4th…Longtime Colt
Player:_________________ Pts:_____

56

1st…"Not Vegas"
2nd…Notre Dame
3rd…1980 rookie
4th…Patriot mistake
Player:_________________ Pts:_____

57

1st…Jets 1995 #1
2nd…"Not Cindy"
3rd…"Not Marsha"
4th…Penn State
Player:_________________ Pts:_____

58

1st…Packers '95 pick
2nd…Rookie record 19 passes defended
3rd…A.S.U.
4th…#21
Player:_________________ Pts:_____

59

1st…8th overall 1999
2nd…Buckeye
3rd…Wide Receiver
4th…"Tea Party"
Player:_________________ Pts:_____

60

1st…Only soph to win Heisman
2nd…QB'd two National Champ teams
3rd…Led Broncos to 2011 playoffs
4th…Kneel down TD celebration
Player:_________________ Pts:_____

61

1st...Badger RB phenom
2nd...NCAA career rushing leader
3rd...Giants #1 pick in 2000
4th...Scooby was a Great ...?
Player:___________________ Pts:_____

62

1st...2nd overall pick in 2006
2nd...1000-yard 'phin
3rd...Trojan hero
4th...A Saint
Player:___________________ Pts:_____

63

1st...Cal RB #1 pick
2nd...Skittles
3rd...Seahawks records holder
4th..."Beast Mode"
Player:___________________ Pts:_____

64

1st...#1 TE pick in 2002
2nd...2002 Rookie of the Year
3rd...Hurricane
4th...Electrical accident
Player:___________________ Pts:_____

65

1st...2005 NFL MVP
2nd...Set NFL record 28 TD's
3rd...5-consecutive 1000 yard seasons
4th...Seahawks #1 Pick
Player:___________________ Pts:_____

66

1st...Early 90's Notre Dame star RB
2nd...Rams #1 Pick
3rd...Steeler 1000-yarder
4th..."The Bus"
Player:___________________ Pts:_____

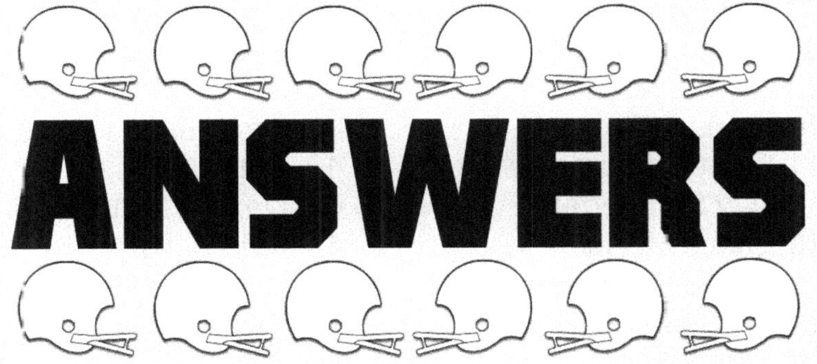
ANSWERS

ANSWERS

QUARTERBACKS

1. Dave Krieg
2. Joe Theisman
3. Bobby Hebert
4. Alex Smith
5. Steve Young
6. Terry Bradshaw
7. Jim Zorn
8. Jim McMahon
9. Bernie Kosar
10. Chris Miller
11. Doug Williams
12. Jay Schroeder
13. Steve McNair
14. Steve DeBerg
15. Elvis Grbac
16. Dan Fouts
17. Kurt Warner
18. Vinny Testeverde
19. John Hadl
20. Jim Everett
21. John Elway
22. Boomer Esiason
23. Rick Mirer
24. Rex Grossman
25. Akili Smith
26. Bubby Brister
27. Joe Namath
28. Scott Mitchell
29. Brian Sipe
30. Andre Ware
31. Don Majkowski
32. Steve Walsh
33. Jack Thompson
34. Donovan McNabb
35. Norm Snead
36. Rodney Peete
37. Jeff Hostetler
38. Adrian McPherson
39. Jim Plunkett
40. Kerry Collins
41. Dan Pastorini
42. Kyle Boller
43. Drew Henson
44. Richard Todd
45. A.J. Feeley
46. Kordell Stewart
47. Neil Lomax
48. Jake Delhomme
49. Roman Gabriel
50. Jim Hart
51. Rob Johnson
52. Shane Matthews
53. Ken Anderson
54. Jeff Blake
55. Tommy Maddox
56. Greg Landry
57. Stan Humphries
58. Cade McNown

 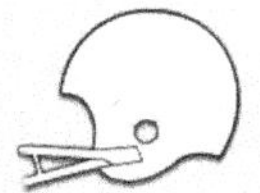

ANSWERS

QUARTERBACKS

59. Don Strock
60. Ron Jaworski
61. Tony Banks
62. Joe Ferguson
63. Danny White
64. Joey Harrington
65. Trent Green
66. Gary Danielson
67. Chuck Long
68. David Klingler
69. Craig Erickson
70. Vince Evans
71. Craig Morton
72. Paul Justin
73. Matt Cassel
74. Dan McGwire
75. Anthony Dilweg
76. Scott Secules
77. Peter Tom Willis
78. Billy Joe Tolliver
79. Dieter Brock
80. Steve Dills
81. Todd Philcox
82. Rick Morton
83. Mark Vlasic
84. Bill Musgrave
85. Steve Pisarkiewicz

ANSWERS

RUNNING BACKS

1. Herschel Walker
2. Kevin Mack
3. Earnest Jackson
4. Bobby Humphrey
5. William Andrews
6. Gary Anderson
7. Fred Taylor
8. Freeman McNeil
9. Lionel James
10. Rueben Mayes
11. Ricky Williams
12. Craig Heyward
13. Ricky Watters
14. George Rogers
15. Jamal Anderson
16. Roger Craig
17. Chris Warren
18. Reggie Cobb
19. Billy Sims
20. Dave Meggett
21. William Henderson
22. Larry Brown
23. Harvey Williams
24. Andra Franklin
25. Otis Armstrong
26. Matt Suhey
27. Bo Jackson
28. Corey Dillon
29. Eric Rhett
30. Tim Worley
31. Thurman Thomas
32. Thomas Jones
33. Pete Johnson
34. Joe Delaney
35. Carnell "Cadillac" Williams
36. Ron Dayne
37. Rod smart
38. Lawrence McCutcheon
39. Priest Holmes
40. Barry Foster
41. Rodney Hampton
42. Todd Collins
43. Tyrone Wheatley
44. Don Woods
45. Curtis Dickey
46. Leroy Kelly
47. Marion Butts
48. John Brockington
49. Mark Van Eeghan
50. Barry Word
51. Tony Dorsett
52. Otis Armstrong
53. Sammie Smith
54. Wendell Tyler
55. Ronnie Brown
56. Reggie Brooks
57. James Wilder
58. Mack Strong

ANSWERS

RUNNING BACKS

59. Lamar Smith
60. John Cappeletti
61. Rocky Bleier
62. Reuben Droughns
63. Harold Green
64. Lydell Mitchell
65. Leroy Hoard
66. Delvin Williams
67. Bruce Harper
68. Erric Pegram
69. Wilbur Jackson
70. Larry Centers
71. Byron "Bam" Morris
72. Keith Woodside
73. Maurice Morris
74. Terdell Middleton
75. Curtis Bledsoe
76. Sherman Smith
77. Tony Reed
78. Rickey Young
79. Walter Abercrombie
80. Billy Jackson
81. Frank Hawkins

ANSWERS

RECEIVERS

1. Wes Welker
2. Raghib Ismail
3. Eric Moulds
4. Nat Moore
5. Chris Carter
6. Steve Largent
7. Fred Belitnekoff
8. Jim Jensen
9. Ozzie Newsome
10. Willie Anderson
11. Louis Lipps
12. Darrell Jackson
13. Ricky Sanders
14. Mervyn Fernandez
15. John Taylor
16. Jake Reed
17. Billy Johnson
18. Anthony Carter
19. Lance Allworth
20. Peter Warrick
21. Roger Carr
22. Joe Horn
23. Haven Moses
24. Ike Harris
25. Stephone Paige
26. Terry Glenn
27. Amani Toomer
28. Ricky Nattiel
29. Ahmad Rashad
30. Tony Hill
31. Sammie White
32. T.J. Houshmandzadeh
33. Braylon Edwards
34. Charlie Taylor
35. Brett Perriman
36. Drew Hill
37. John Stallworth
38. Anthony Miller
39. Paul Warfield
40. Webster Slaughter
41. John Jefferson
42. O.J. McDuffie
43. Cliff Branch
44. Ernest Givins
45. Bill Brooks
46. Wesley walker
47. Kevin House
48. Rob Moore
49. Calvin Johnson
50. Bert Emanuel
51. Herman Moore
52. Rod Smith
53. Andre Johnson
54. Ben Coates
55. Jimmy Smith
56. Matt Jones
57. Ed McCaffrey
58. Brandon Stokley

ANSWERS

RECEIVERS

59. Eddie Brown
60. Johnny Rodgers
61. Keenan McCardell
62. Eddie Kennison
63. Harold Carmichael
64. Antonio Freeman
65. J.J. Stokes
66. Jaquez Green
67. Greg Jennings
68. Jimmie Giles
69. Curtis Conway
70. Tim McGee
71. Mark Duper
72. Joe Senser
73. Billy Brooks
74. Louis Clark
75. Buster Rhymes
76. Horrace Copeland
77. Jimmy Ceffalo
78. Howard Twilley
79. Lake Dawson
80. Tim Smith
81. Brian Baschnagel
82. Mike Pritchard
83. Sidney Rice
84. Drew Pearson
85. Hines Ward
86. Carl Roaches

ANSWERS

DEFENSE

1. Ed Reed
2. William Perry
3. Frank Minnifield
4. Merlin Olsen
5. Joe Greene
6. Mark Gastineau
7. Hugh Green
8. Lavar Arrington
9. Ted Hendricks
10. Jevon Kearse
11. Brian Jordan
12. Percy Snow
13. Deron Cherry
14. Broderick Thomas
15. Deion Sanders
16. Rod Woodson
17. Mike Singletary
18. Dave Brown
19. A.J. Hawk
20. Tony Woods
21. Leroy Irvin
22. Cornelius Bennett
23. Raymond Clayborn
24. Warren Sapp
25. Terrell Buckley
26. Carnell Lake
27. Sam Adams
28. Lawyer Milloy
29. Gary Fencik
30. Marty Lyons
31. Zach Thomas
32. Joe Lavender
33. Ross Browner
34. Kevin Greene
35. Gary Johnson
36. Chris Spielman
37. Bryan Cox
38. Art Still
39. Frank LeMaster
40. Aneas Williams
41. Chris Zorich
42, Tommy Hart
43. Cortez Kennedy
44. Clay Matthews
45. Wally Chambers
46. Bryant Young
47. Joe Klecko
48. Matt Blair
49. Robert Brazile
50. Aaron Glenn
51. Keith Bulluck
52. Fred Dean
53. Terence Newman
54. Richard Dent

ANSWERS

FOOTBALL FAMILIES

1. Mosi Tatupu
2. Bill Kenney
3. Chris Simms
4. Eric Metcalf
5. Mike Thomas
6. Qudry Ismail
7. Mike Renfro
8. Sterling Sharpe
9. Lee Roy Selmon
10. Don Hasselbeck
11. Joe Morris
12. Brian Blades
13. Greg & Mike Pruitt
14. Bob & Brian Griese
15. Chuck Muncie
16. Kellen Winslows'
17. Ronde & Tiki Barber
18. J.K. McKay
19. Babineaux
20. Fritsch's
21. Pete & Stan Brock
22. Monte & Terry Jackson
23. Rashaan Salaam
24. Brian Brohm
25. Rich & Ron Saul
26. Marion Barbers'
27. Kinchens
28. Todd Marinovich
29. Springs
30. McCowns'
31. Nate & Tim Newton
32. Darren & Jamie Sharper
33. Shulas'
34. John & Mike Tice
35. Zendejas
36. Matthews

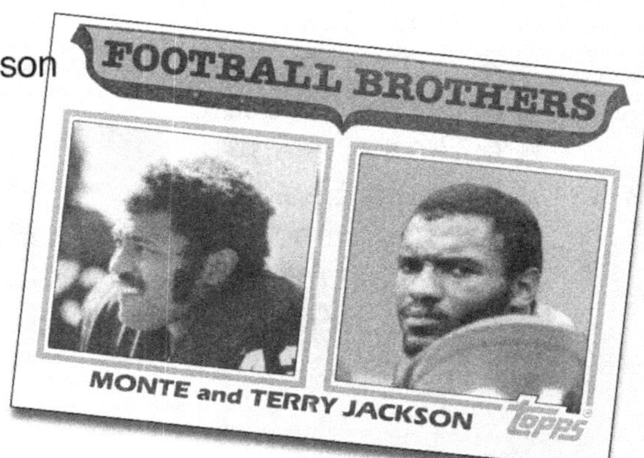

ANSWERS

1 PICKS

1. Tony Eason
2. Hart Lee Dykes
3. Blair Thomas
4. Keyshawn Johnson
5. Patrick Bates
6. Garrison Hearst
7. Bruce Smith
8. Andre Rison
9. Tye Hill
10. Chuck Long
11. Dexter Carter
12. Heath Shuler
13. D.J. Dozier
14. John L. Williams
15. Jim Druckenmiller
16. Keith Byars
17. Louis Oliver
18. Lawrence Phillips
19. Al Toon
20. Timm Rosenbach
21. A.J. Duhe
22. Tommy Kramer
23. Steve Broussard
24. Brad Muster
25. Kenny Easley
26. Russ Francis
27. Phil Simms
28. Carson Palmer
29. Ed Jones
30. Michael Clayton
31. Kellen Winslow
32. Reggie Wayne
33. Ken Burrough
34. Art Monk
35. John Copeland
36. Ottis Anderson
37. Greg Bell
38. Ricky Bell
39. Jacob Green
40. Otis Armstrong
41. Leonard Renfro
42. Mike Haynes
43. Jack Reynolds
44. George Teague
45. Drew Bledsoe
46. Terence Newman
47. Tony Gonzalez
48. Barty Smith
49. Barry Smith
50. Keith Brooking
51. Tamba Hali
52. Napoleon Kaufman
53. Darrin Nelson
54. Chris Singleton
55. Bert Jones
56. Vagas Ferguson
57. Kyle Brady
58. Craig Newsome

ANSWERS

1 PICKS

59. David Boston
60. Tim Tebow
61. Ron Dayne
62. Reggie Bush
63. Marshawn Lynch
64. Jeremy Shockey
65. Shaun Alexander
66. Jeome Bettis

 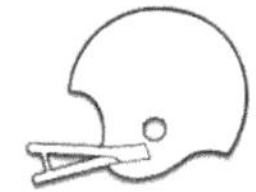

THANKS

94

Special thanks to the Topps Company, Inc. They serve as the inspiration, dedication and celebration of this project. They have continually put out the best trading cards for decades, setting the gold standard year after year for enthusiasts, and geeks like me. Topps is single-handedly responsible for teaching me the art of collecting, and has bonded my friends, family and I with a common hobby for a lifetime.